100 Things For Toddlers & Kids coloring Book

Copyright © 2018 Adriana P. Jenova

First edition: First printing
Illustrations and design © 2018 Adriana P. Jenova

Author Contact

Facebook page : www.facebook.com/Adrianapjenovacoloringbook

This Book Belong To:

OCTOPUS

PUFFERFISH

DOLPHIN

FISH

BOOK

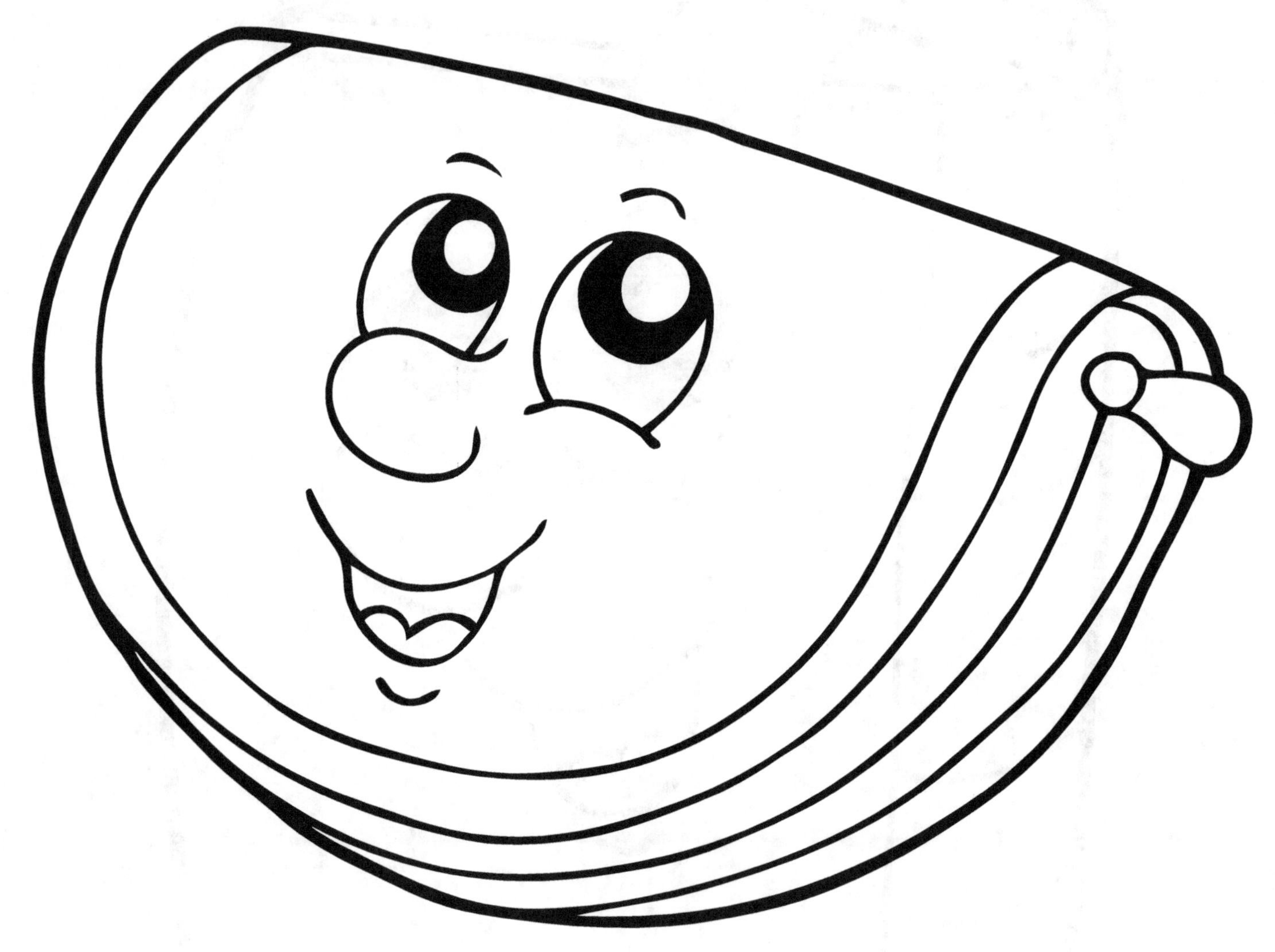

PENCIL BAG

PENCIL CASE

PENCIL

RULER

SCHOOLBAG

DRAWER

VASE

MIRROR

LAMP

SOFA

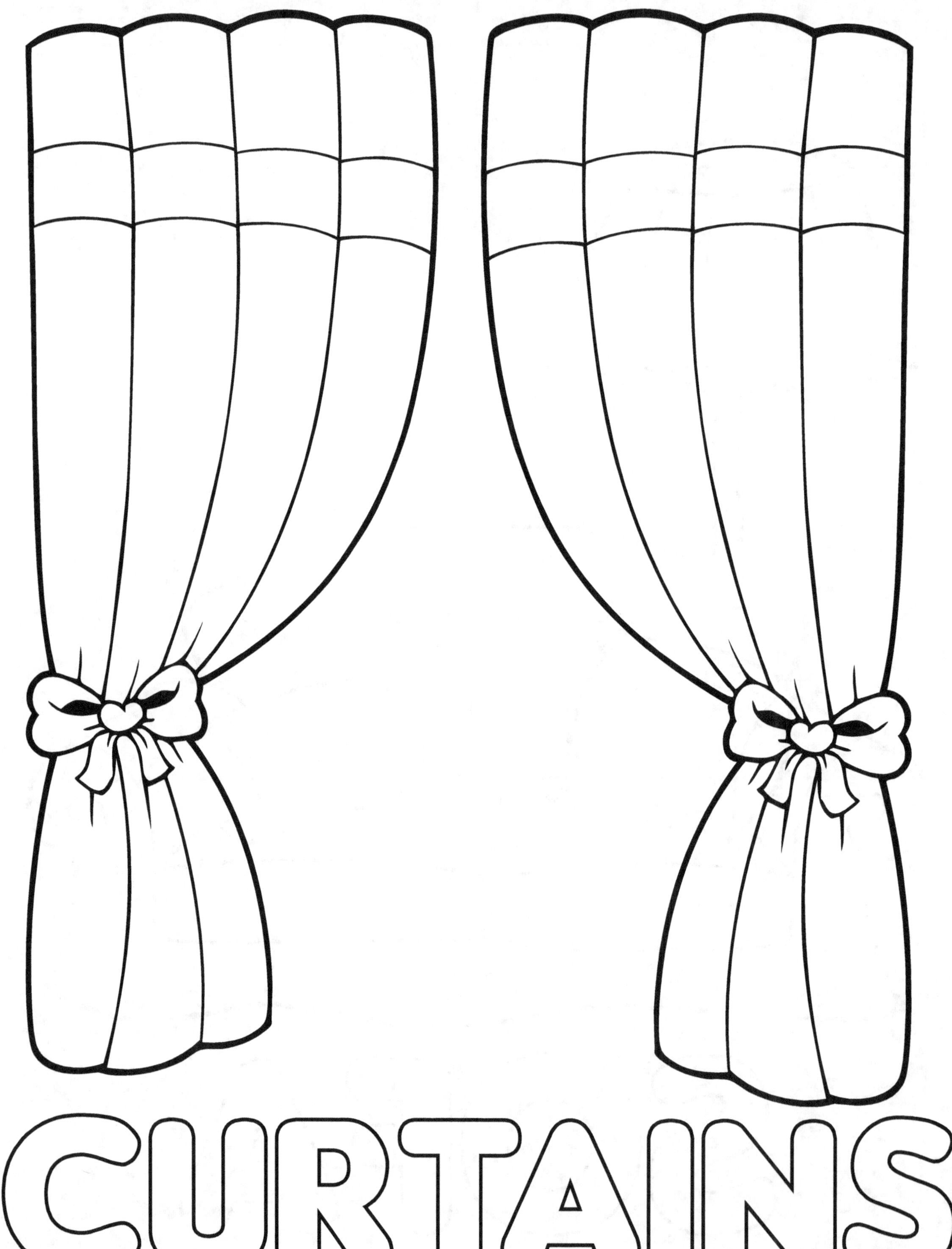

CURTAINS

BASKET

WATERINGCAN

HAT

RABBIT

TEDDY BEAR

TRUCK

AIRPLANE

TRAIN

ROBOT

HELICOPTER

HOME

WHALE

SEAL

CLOWNFISH

STINGRAY

PRAWN

POMEGRANATES

LEMONS

APPLES

MELON

WATERMELON

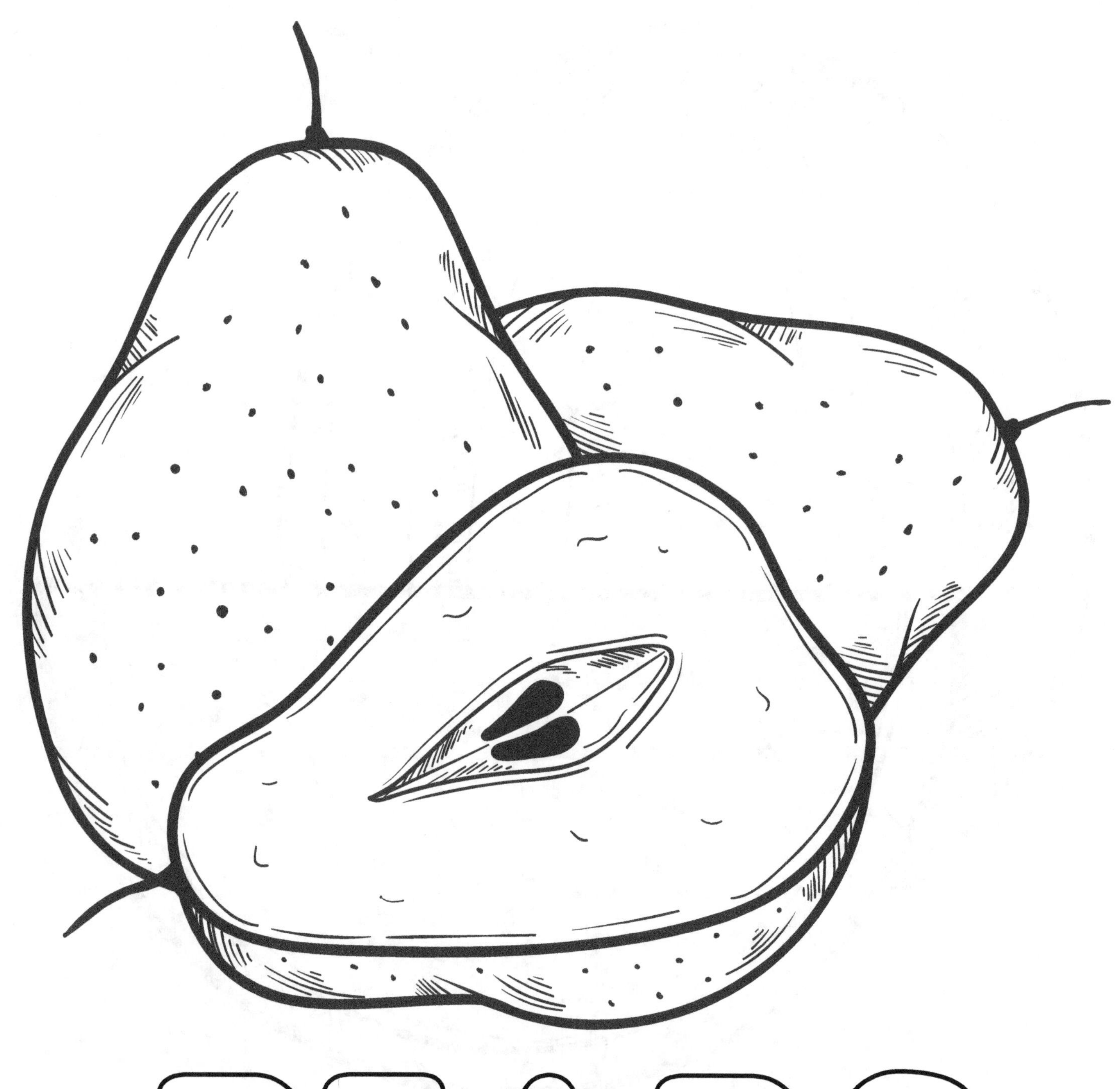

PEARS

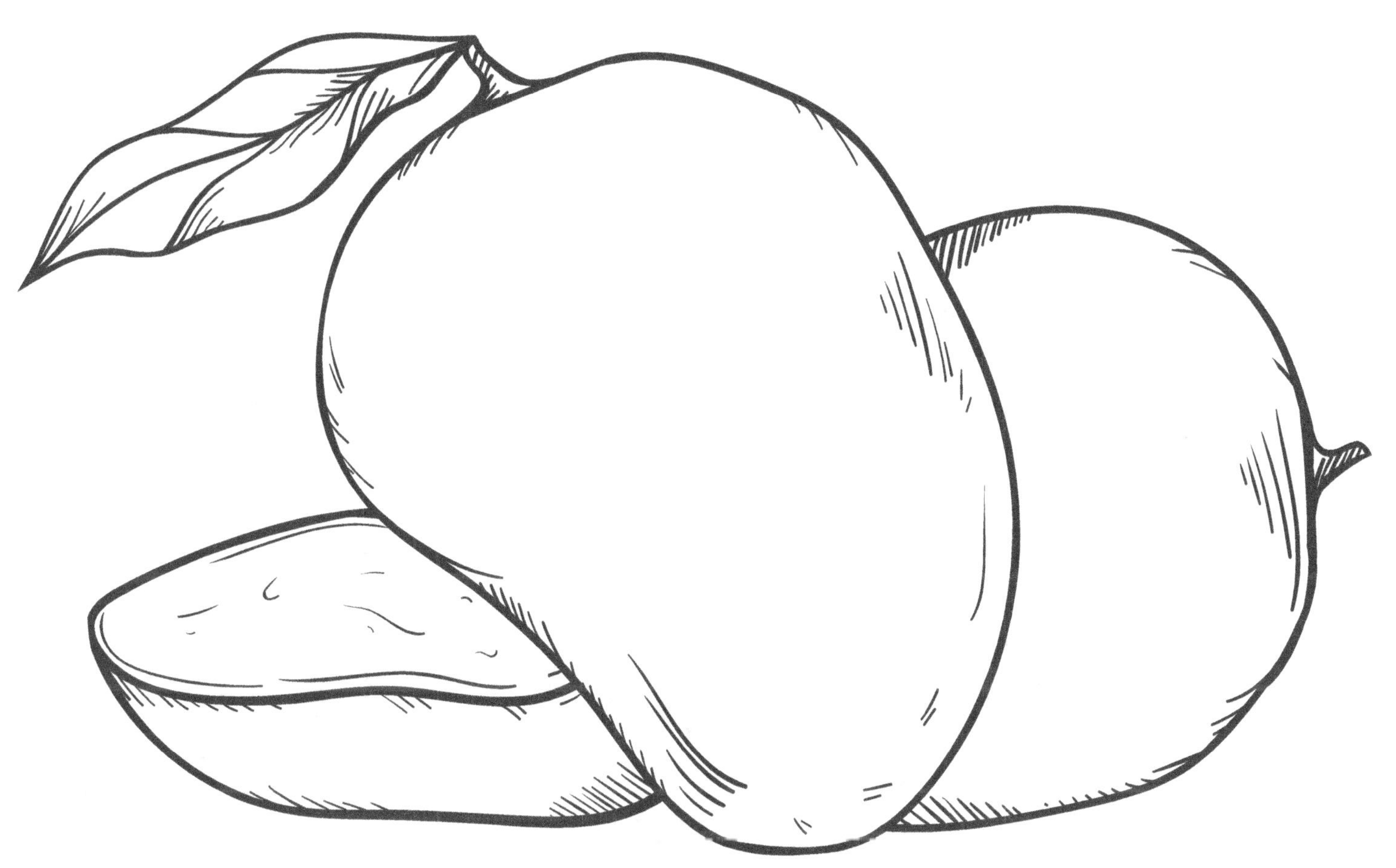

MANGOS

PINEAPPLE

STRAWBERRYS

BROCCOLI

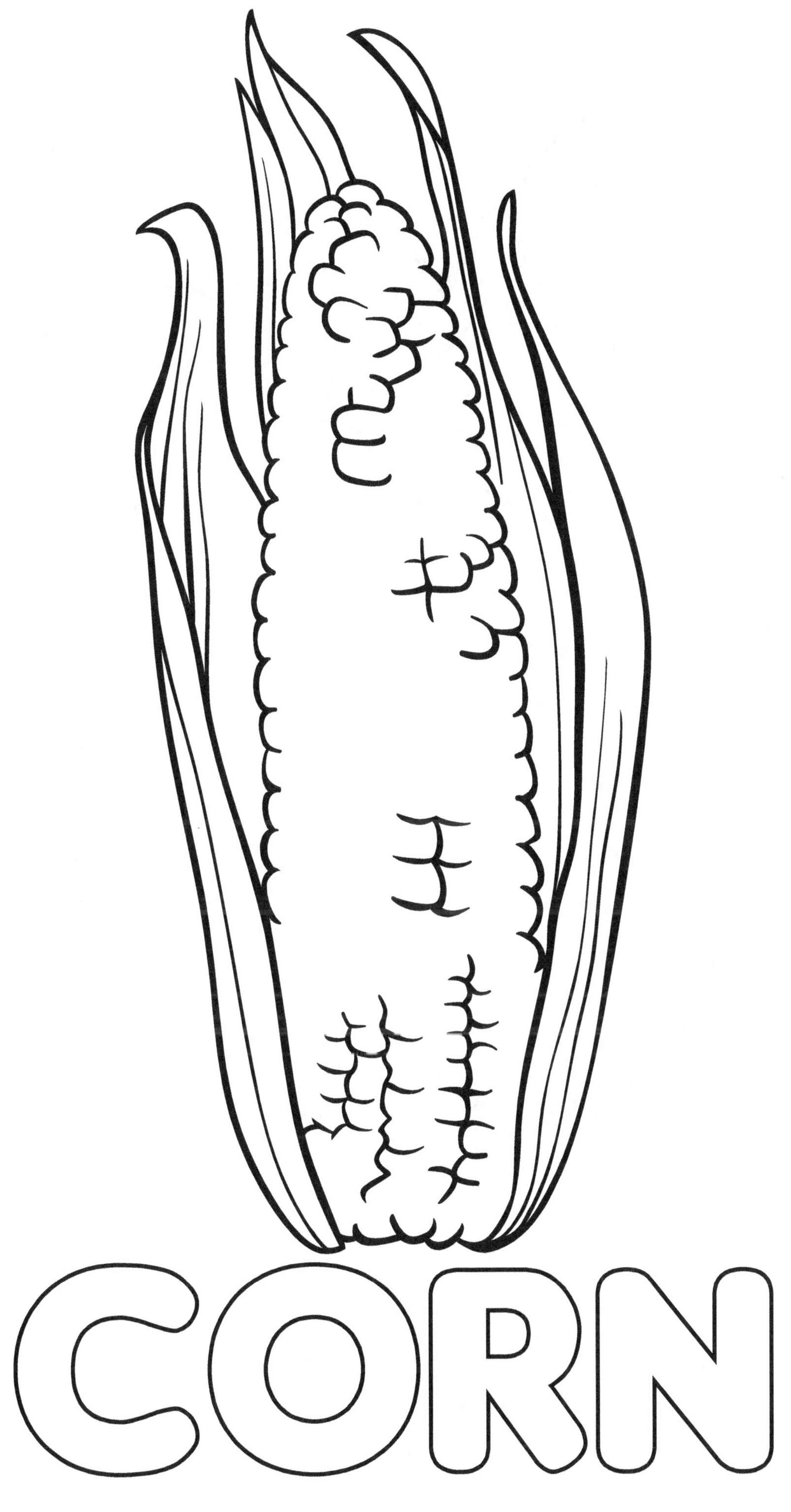

CORN

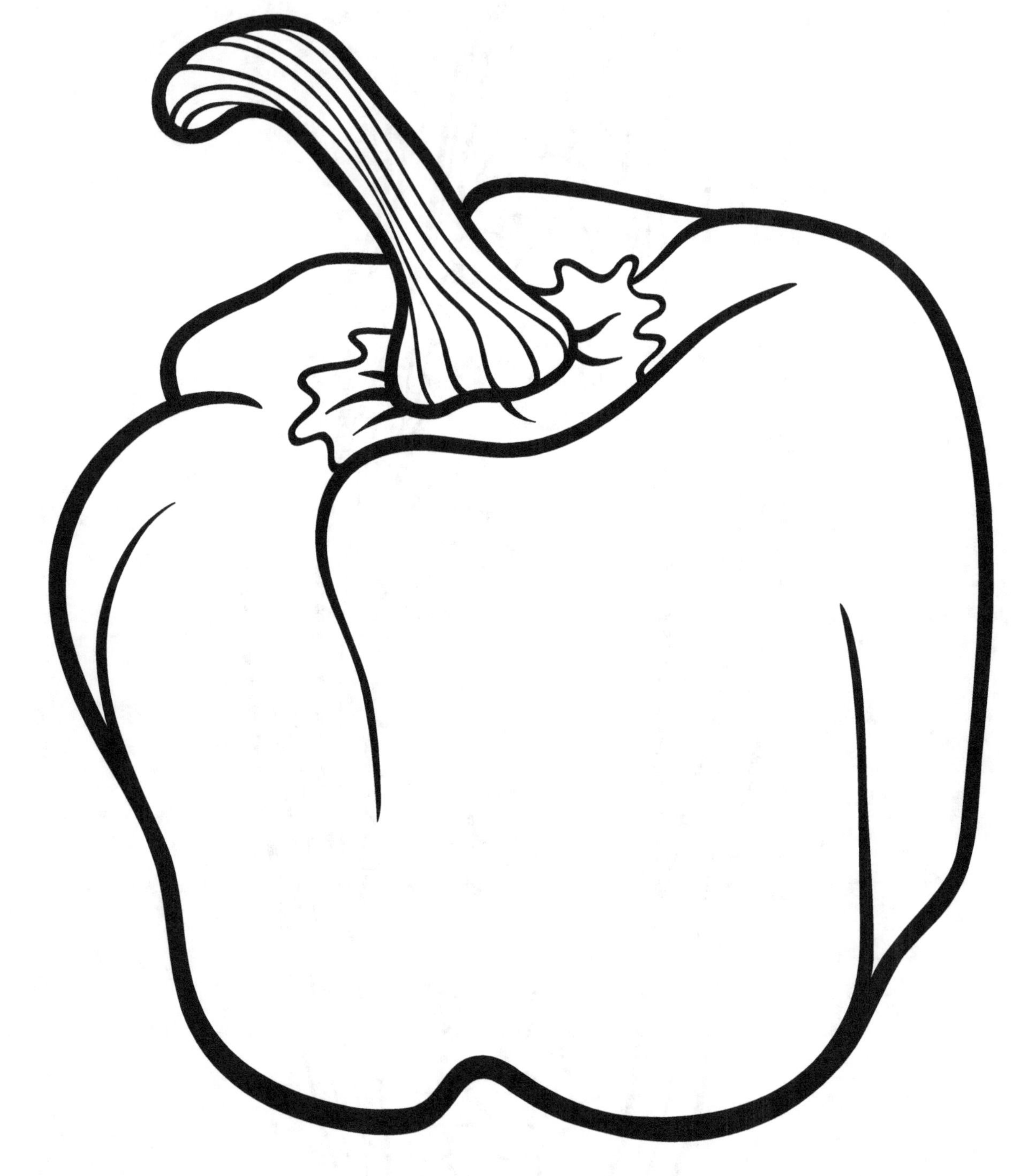

CAPSICUM

CABBAGE

TOMATO

ONION

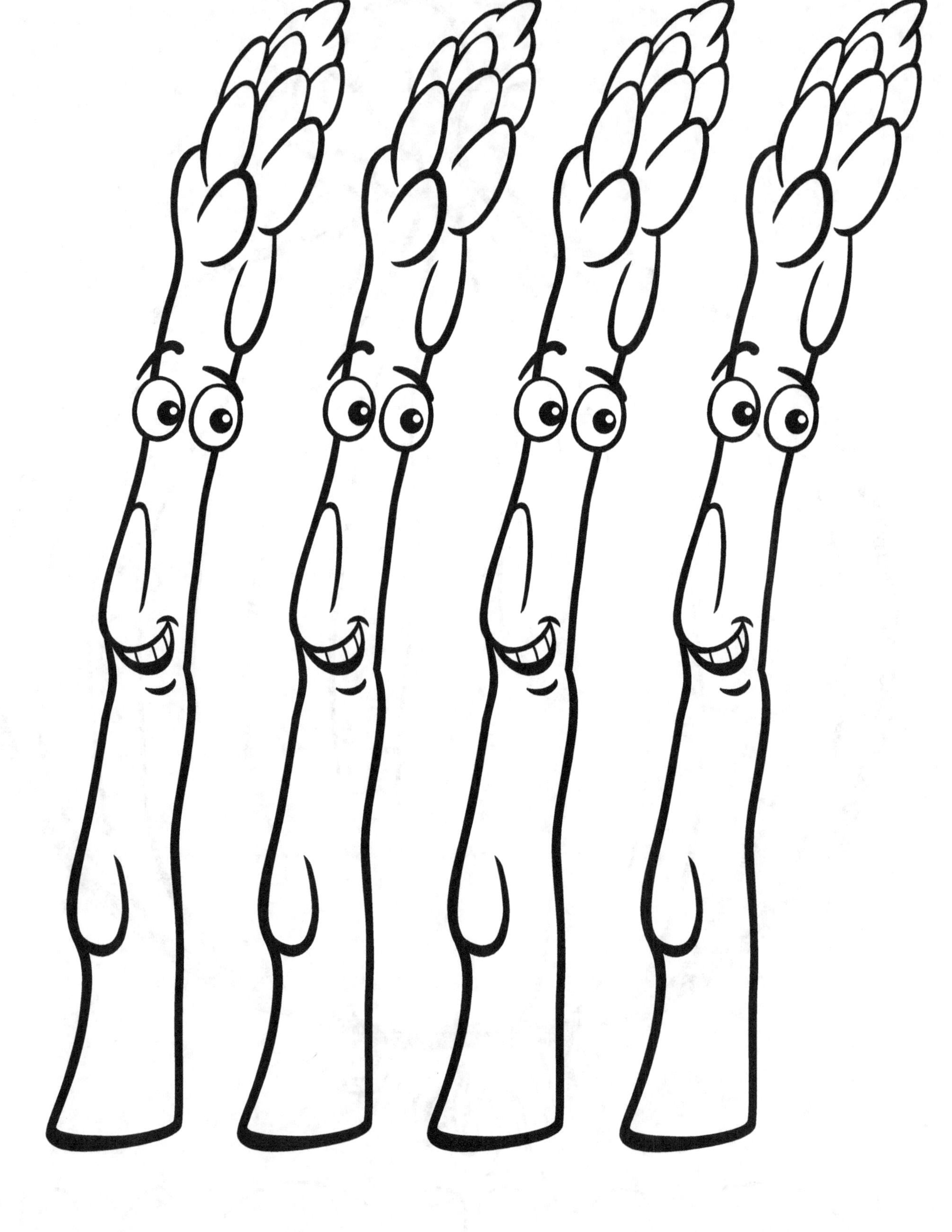

ASPARAGUS

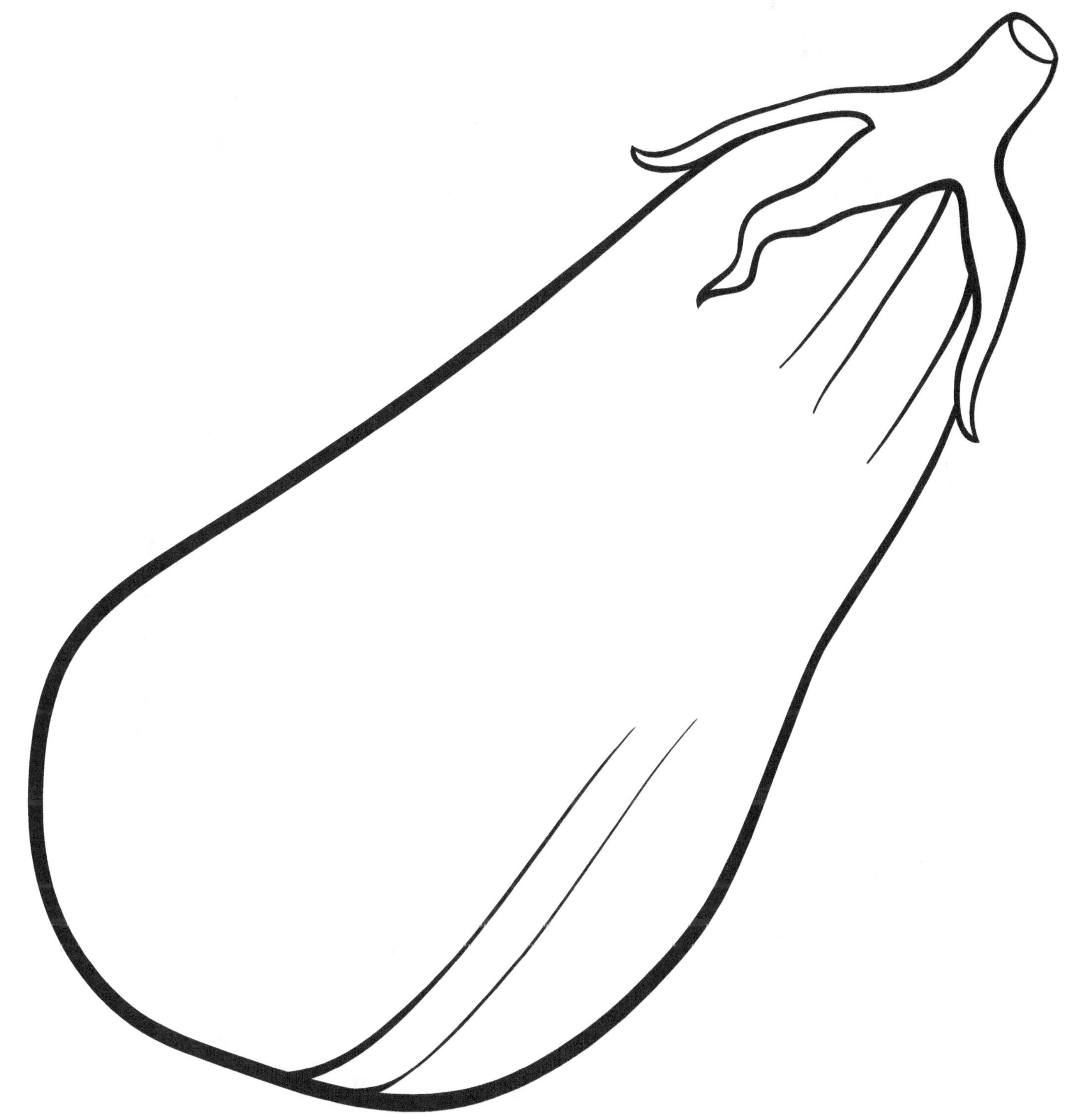

EGGPLANT

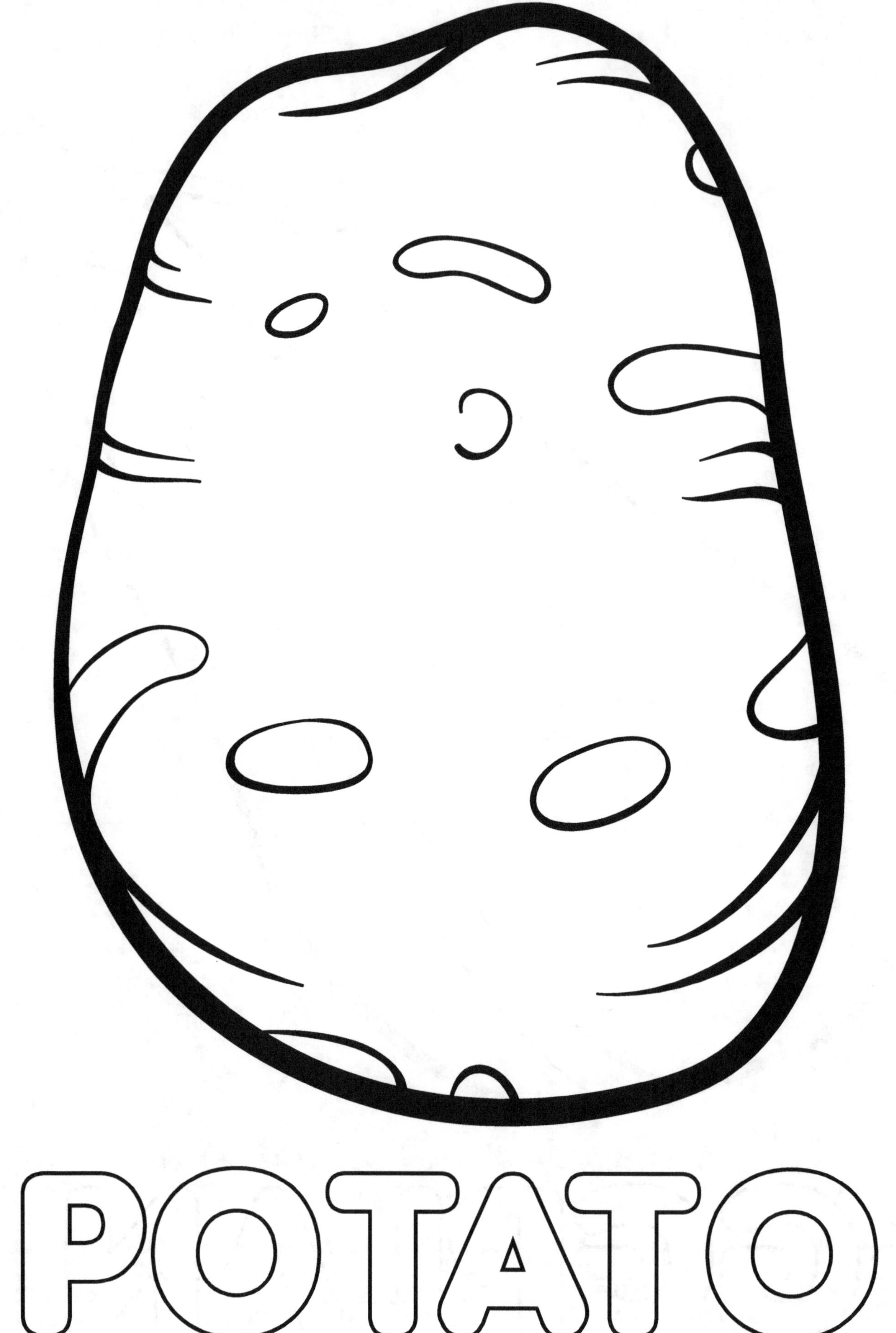

POTATO

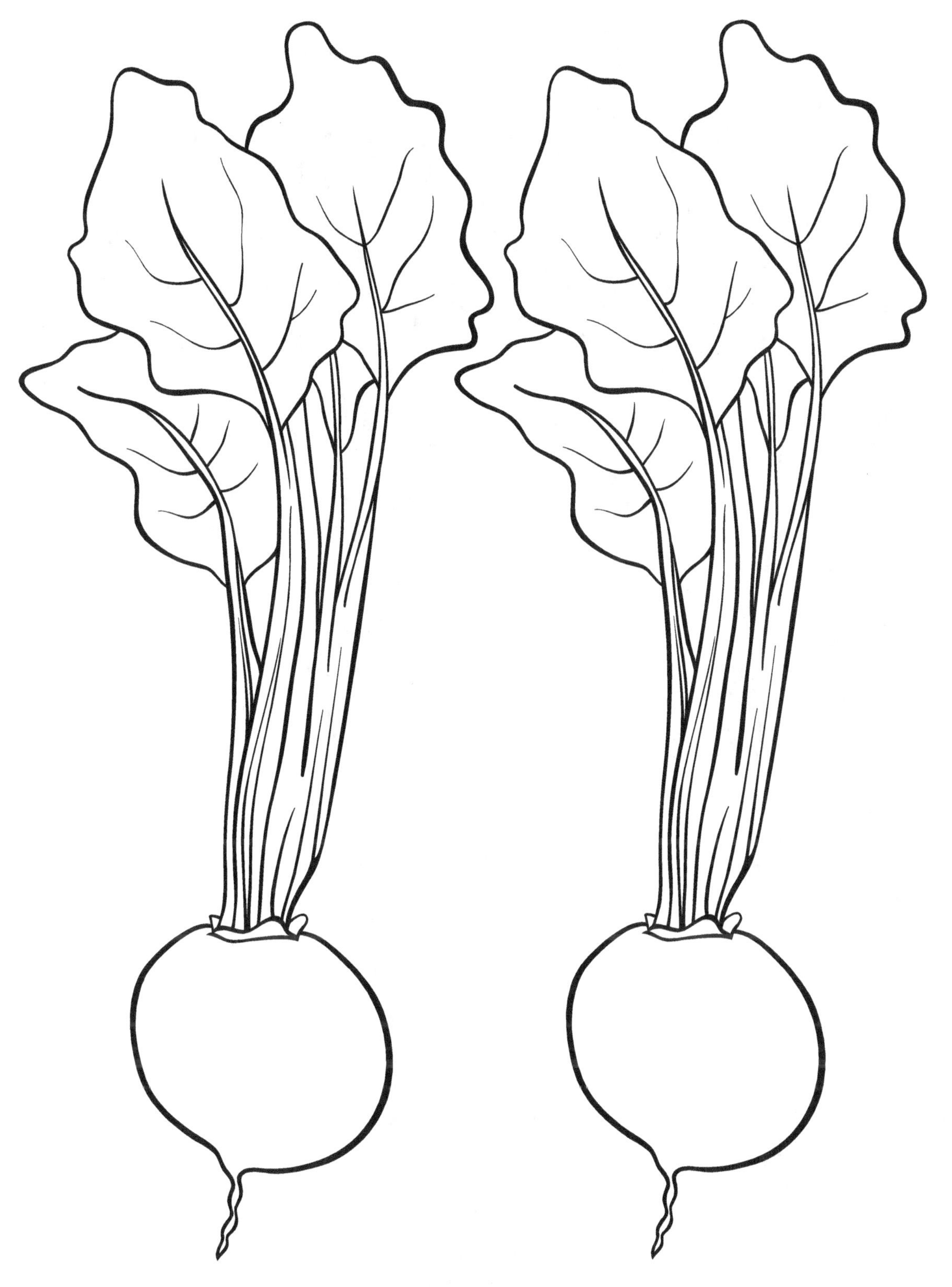

BEETROOTS

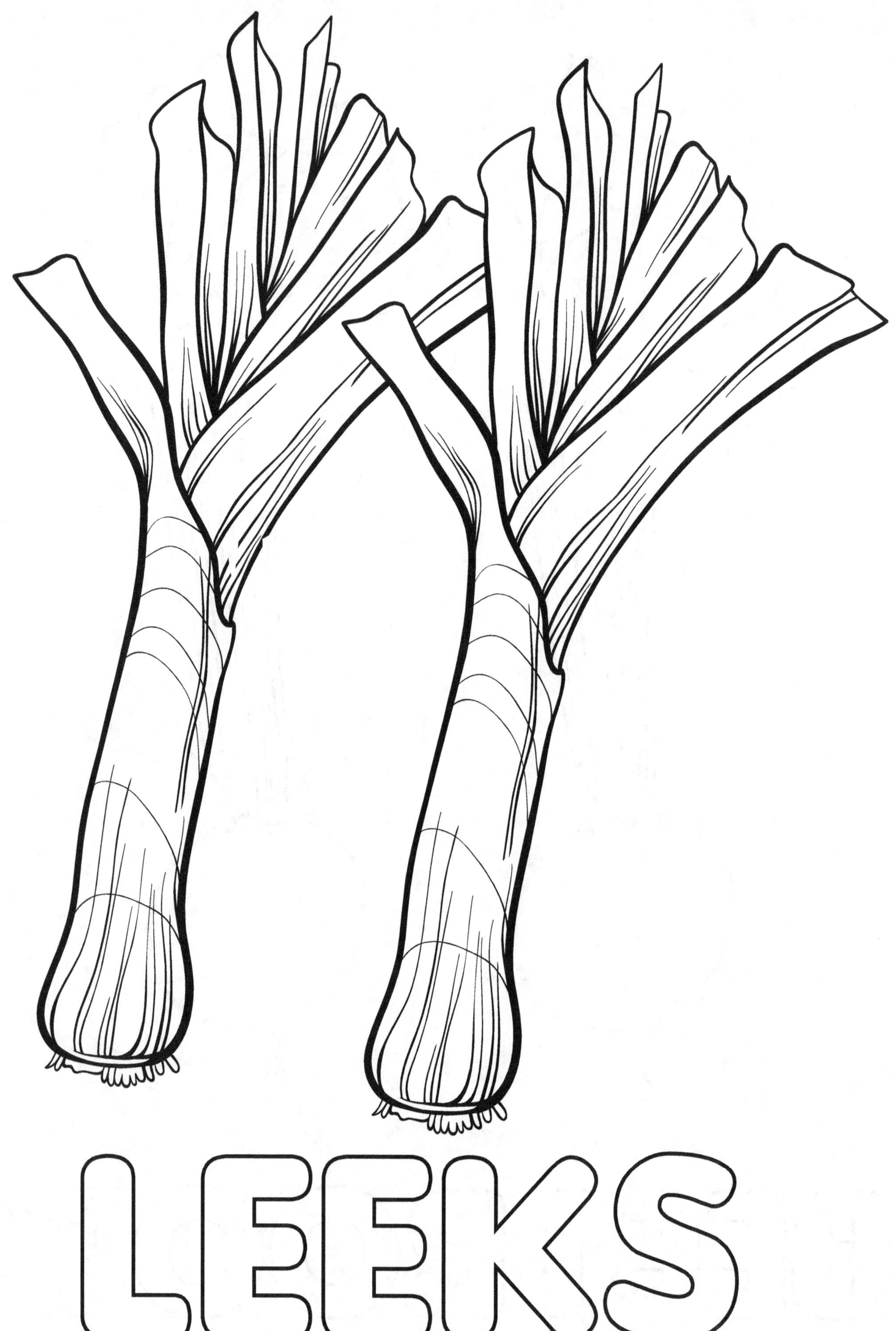
LEEKS

CARROTS

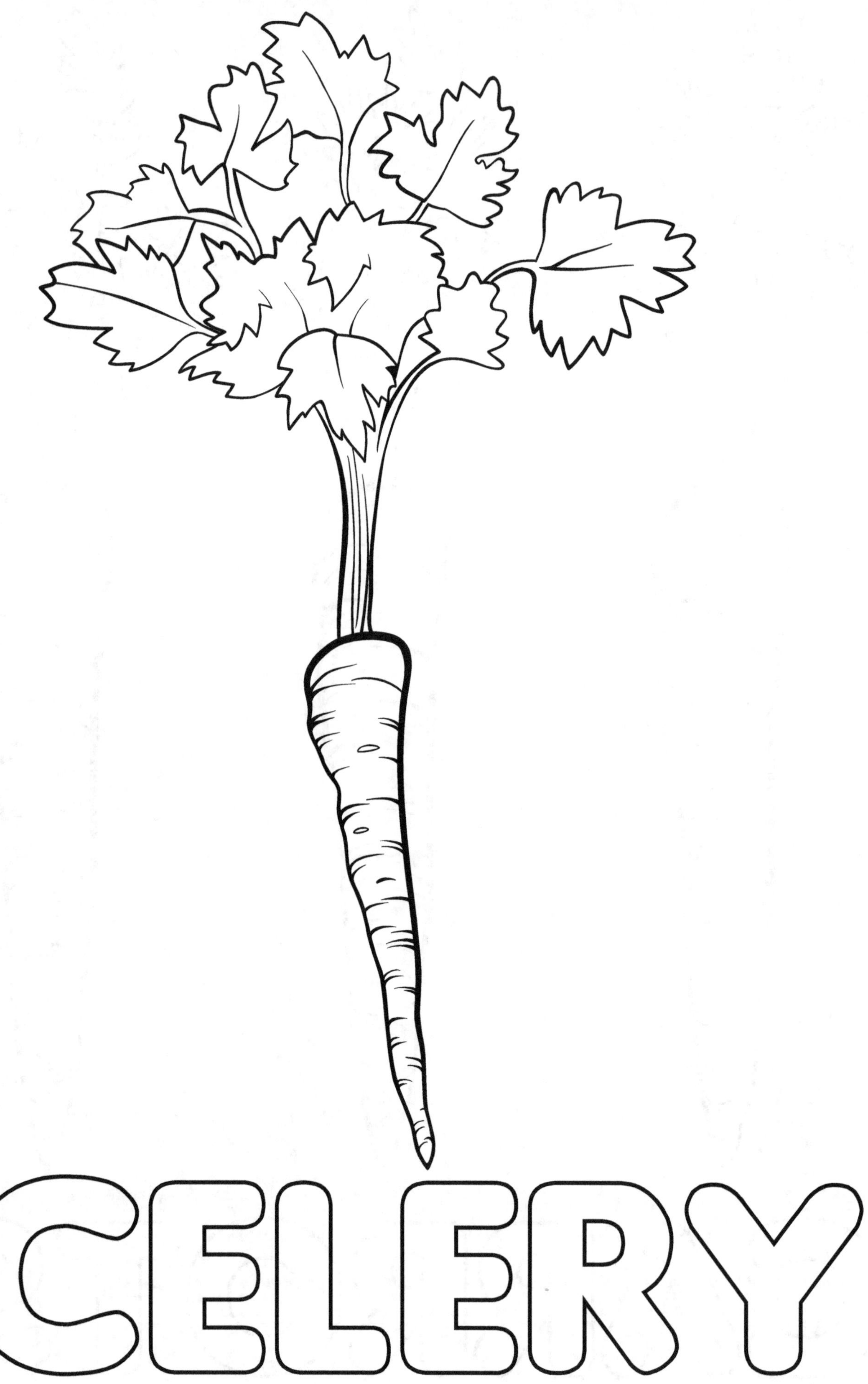

CELERY

CAKE

BAKERY

PIRATE

TURTLE

SNAIL

WORMS

BANANAS

PIRATE SHIP

PIRATE TREASURES

SHARK

SANTA CLAUS

GIFTS

DOGS

PENGUIN

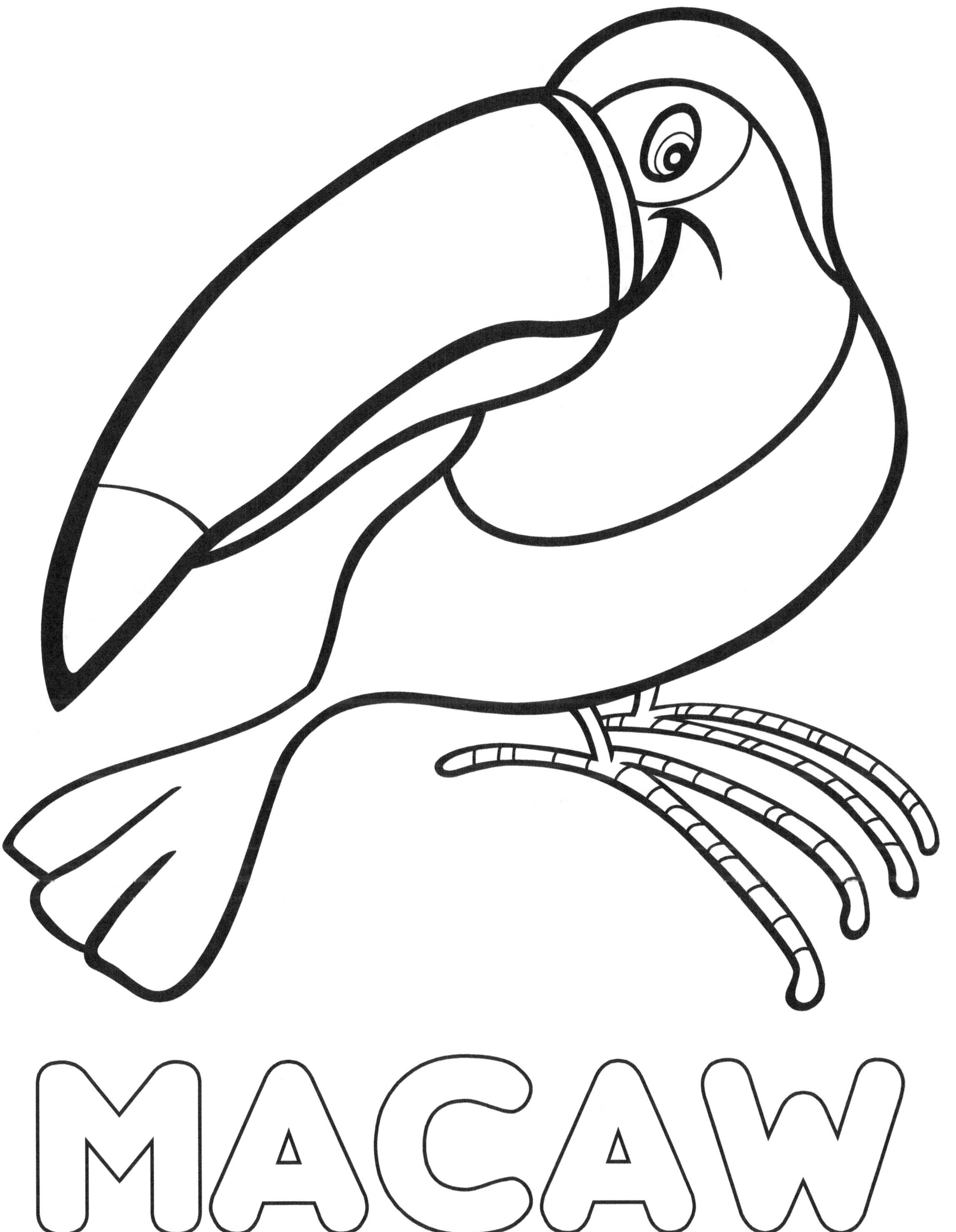

MACAW

RAT

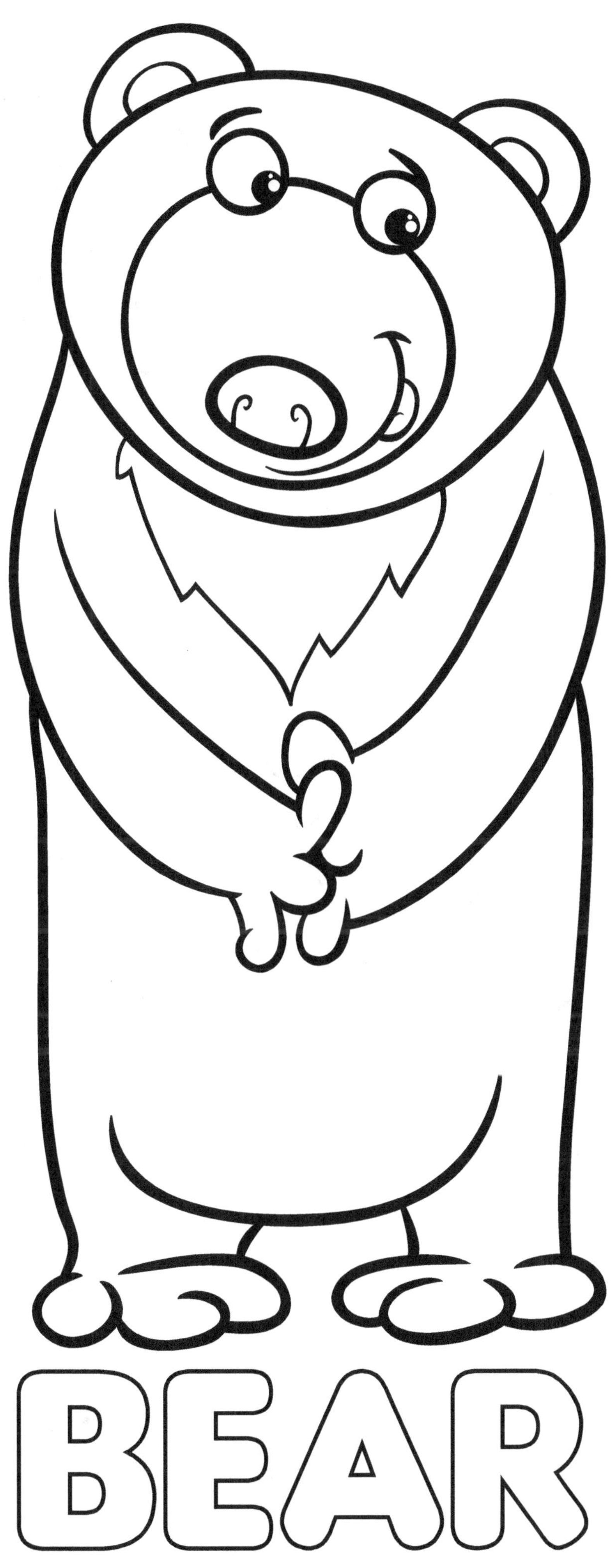

BEAR

DINOSAUR

KIDS

BOY CLOTHES

GIRL CLOTHES

PRINCESS

CAT

FAIRY BOY

FAIRY

CLOCK

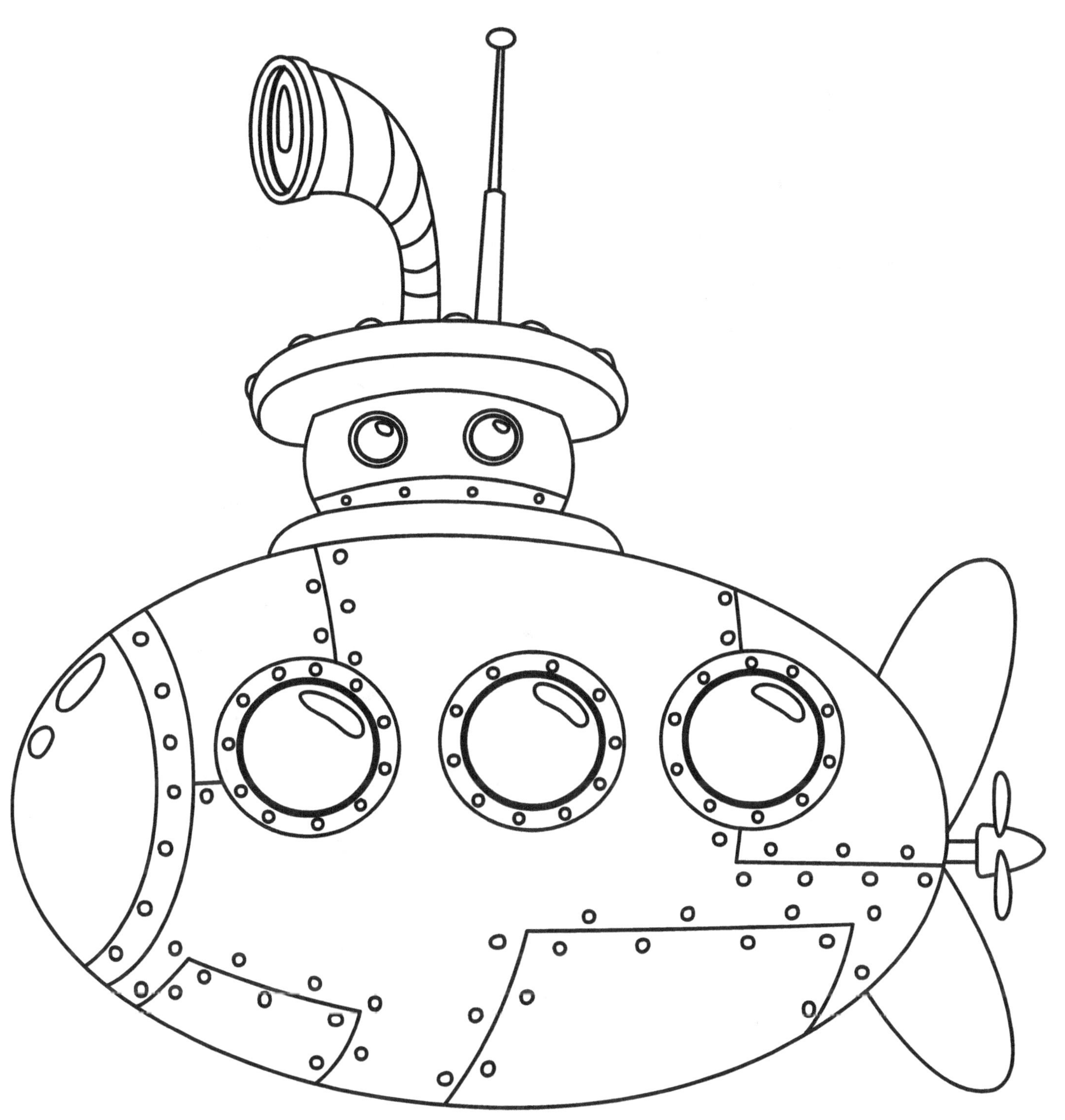

SUBMARINE

CHICKEN

SCHOOL BUS

REINDEER

WITCH

PIG

OWL

MONKEY

ELEPHANT